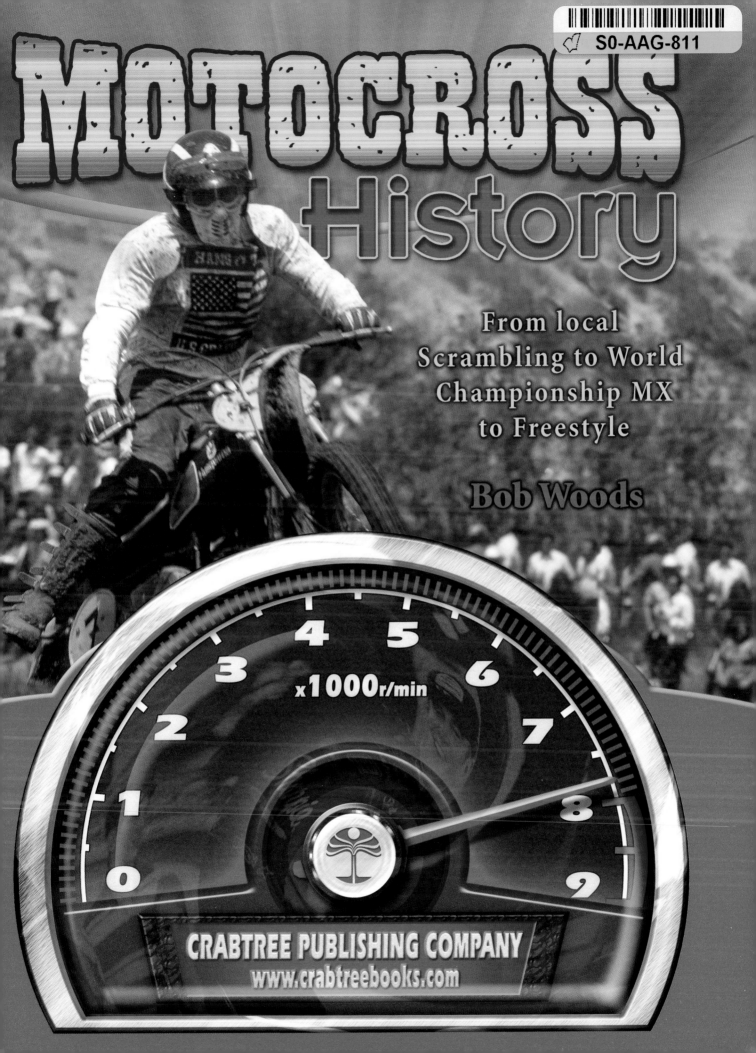

MOTOCROSS History

From local
Scrambling to World
Championship MX
to Freestyle

Bob Woods

x**1000**r/min

CRABTREE PUBLISHING COMPANY
www.crabtreebooks.com

Crabtree Publishing Company

www.crabtreebooks.com

Coordinating editor: Chester Fisher
Series and project editor: Shoreline Publishing Group LLC
Author: Jim Gigliotti
Series Consultant: Bryan Stealey
Project Manager: Kavita Lad
Art direction: Rahul Dhiman
Design: Ranjan Singh
Cover Design: Ranjan Singh
Photo research: Akansha Srivastava
Editors: Adrianna Morganelli, Mike Hodge

Acknowledgments

The publishers would like to thanks the following for permission to reproduce photographs:

p4: Simon Cudby (all); p5: Simon Cudby; p6: Joachim Köhler/Deutsches Zweirad- und NSU-Museum; p7: British Army Photographer\Imperial War Museum; p8: Simon Cudby; p10: Hulton-Deutsch Collection/CORBIS; p11: Hulton-Deutsch Collection/CORBIS; p12: McGregor/Getty Images; p13: Topical Press Agency/Getty Images (top); p13: Ronald Startup/Getty Images (bottom); p14: Grundy/Getty Images; p15: Douglas Miller/Getty Images (top); p15: Central Press/ Getty Images (bottom); p16: Harry Todd/Stringer/Getty Images; p17: ASSOCIATED PRESS; p18: Terry Good Collection; p19: Paul Webb Photography; p20: Paul Webb Photography; p21: Terry Good Collection; p22: Simon Cudby; p23: Terry Good Collection; p24:Terry Good Collection; p25: Simon Cudby; p26: Simon Cudby; p27: Simon Cudby; p28: Simon Cudby (all); p30: Simon Cudby; p31: Simon Cudby (all)

Cover and title page image by Paul Webb Photography

Library and Archives Canada Cataloguing in Publication

Woods, Bob
    Motocross history / Bob Woods.

(MXplosion!)
Includes index.
ISBN 978-0-7787-3987-6 (bound).--ISBN 978-0-7787-4000-1 (pbk.)

1. Motocross--History--Juvenile literature. I. Title. II. Series.

GV1060.12.W66 2008   j796.7'56   C2008-901519-3

Library of Congress Cataloging-in-Publication Data

Woods, Bob.
    Motocross history / Bob Woods.
        p. cm. -- (MXplosion!)
    Includes index.
    ISBN-13: 978-0-7787-4000-1 (pbk. : alk. paper)
    ISBN-10: 0-7787-4000-5 (pbk. : alk. paper)
    ISBN-13: 978-0-7787-3987-6 (reinforced library binding : alk. paper)
    ISBN-10: 0-7787-3987-2 (reinforced library binding : alk. paper)
    1. Motocross--History--Juvenile literature. I. Title.
    GV1060.12.W66 2008
    796.7'56--dc22
                                                          2008009807

Crabtree Publishing Company

www.crabtreebooks.com   1-800-387-7650

Published in Canada
Crabtree Publishing
616 Welland Ave.
St. Catharines, ON
L2M 5V6

Published in the United States
Crabtree Publishing
PMB16A
350 Fifth Ave., Suite 3308
New York, NY 10118

Published in the United Kingdom
Crabtree Publishing
White Cross Mills
High Town, Lancaster
LA1 4XS

Published in Australia
Crabtree Publishing
386 Mt. Alexander Rd.
Ascot Vale (Melbourne)
VIC 3032

Contents

Ready...Set...Go!

Forty motorcycle riders line up for the start of a motocross race. The roar is deafening as they rev their engines. The gate drops, and they're off! Into the first turn they go, sliding into the berm. Every racer knows that it's important to get out in front right away—or risk falling too far behind in the spray of dirt, mud, and grass.

Wheel-to-Wheel Racing

Later on in the race, Ricky Carmichael and James "Bubba" Stewart come flying off a rise in the course, more than 10 feet (3.05 m) in the air. Carmichael and Stewart are two of the best motocross riders of the 2000s. They accelerate out of a **hairpin turn**, and Stewart cuts inside of Carmichael to take the lead. But Ricky knows only one way to race, and that's all-out! He retakes the lead on the next jump. Who will win the race?

(right) AMA Motocross champ Grant Langston gets some big air!

Motocross riders race in the dirt, but numerous jumps on the tracks also let them soar through the air.

European Roots

Motocross is an exciting sport with a vocabulary that's as colorful as the protective equipment that each rider wears. Riders race hard for the "holeshot" (the lead through the first turn after the start), soar through the "whoops" (rows of dirt mounds), and "pin it" (go full throttle) out of the last turn. Those are all modern American terms, but motocross did not begin in the United States. In fact, it came here from Europe, where its roots date to the 1920s, and where it became immensely popular long before it caught on with more than a small segment of sports fans in the United States. Read on, and we'll learn all about motocross's roots and how it got to where it is today—don't forget your helmet!

Two of the best: Seven-time champ Ricky Carmichael (4) battles up-and-coming superstar James Stewart (7).

Word Play

The word "motocross" comes from France. It's a combination of "moto" for motorcycle and "cross" for cross-country. But don't let that fool you into thinking that the French invented the sport! We'll learn later that for a long time, the origin of the word did cause such confusion. But thanks to the work of historians such as Bryan Stealey, we now know that motocross actually started in Great Britain as "scrambling" before it was **exported** to the rest of the world and became "motocross."

The Motorcycle and Motorcycle Racing

When was the first automobile race? Well, Henry Ford (the founder of the Ford Motor Company) once said that it was when the second automobile was built. The same could certainly be said for motorcycle racing.

Before There Was Motocross

What Henry Ford meant was that human nature was sure to take over with two vehicles side by side. "My motorcycle is faster than your motorcycle!" the second motorcycle owner surely said to the first. Or maybe it was the other way around. In any case, motorcycle racing has been with us since the earliest motorcycles were built. And that means that motorcycle racing came long before motocross as we know it began in the 1920s.

Early Motor Bikes

The first motorcycle dates to 1885, when German inventors pretty much put an engine on a bicycle. By the late 1800s, motorcycles were available to the general public, and in the early 1900s, they began to take on characteristics that were more **distinct** from the bicycle. Likewise, motocross bikes eventually began to take on characteristics more distinct from a regular motorcycle. The earliest motocross bikes in the era before World War II (1939-1945) were essentially regular motorcycles.

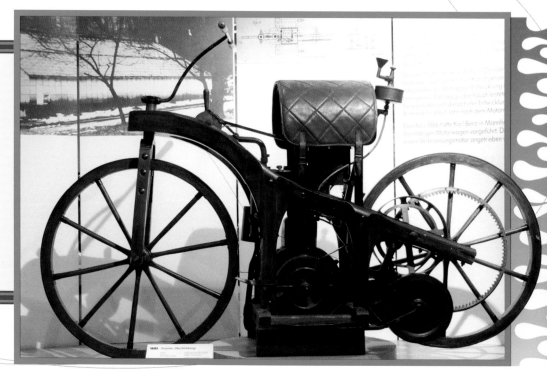

The "bone crusher," a very early motorized bicycle, got its name from the rattling ride allowed by these all-metal wheels.

But riders soon realized that they needed lighter, yet more powerful, bikes to drive over rough terrain. As the sport became more popular, manufacturers met their wishes.

What Makes it Motocross?

Motorcycle races include a variety of different types, from those raced on standard ovals and flat tracks to the off-road races of motocross and **supercross**. Motocross is a closed-course competition that's held over natural terrain, complete with obstacles and hills. Supercross is held over a similar, man-made course inside a large stadium.

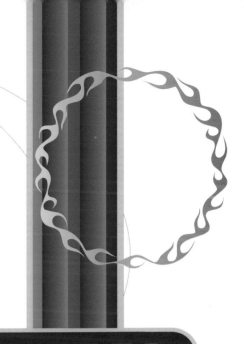

War and Peace

Modern warfare has gone largely high-tech these days, with **sophisticated** weapons, surveillance equipment, and wireless communication. But think back to the early 1900s. World War I, which was fought in Europe and Asia beginning in 1914, was a land war fought in the trenches. How were troops transported over uneven terrain? How did word get from commanders and spies to the front lines? Well, one way was via motorcycle. Small, rugged, and powerful, they could get to places faster and more efficiently than other vehicles could. When the War was over in 1918, lots of troops wanted to keep riding for the fun of it. That was good for the motorcycle business!

British messengers sped through the countrysides of Europe during World War I, using motorcycles to get the job done fast!

Early Trials

Motocross racing can trace its origins to trials competitions on the motorcycle. The most famous of these trials was the Scott Trial, which was founded by Alfred Angus Scott in Britain in the early 1900s.

Make Your Own Road

Early motorcycle riders had to get really good at driving through rough terrain and over and around natural obstacles. That's because they just didn't have nice paved roads to take them from place to place—if they could find any roads at all! Often, they would come to ground that was so muddy and impassable that they had to carry their motorcycles. When they got back to ground they could ride on, they put down the bikes and hit the gas. Naturally, at some point, there were arguments about who was the best rider. The best rider didn't mean the fastest rider. To figure out who was the best rider, trials were born. In a trial competition, the winner was the rider who made the fewest mistakes while completing a course in the shortest time. Judges were stationed at various points of the track to observe the riders. Trials became very popular in motorcycle clubs throughout Britain. The annual Scott Trial was an important event in Northern England by the 1920s.

Company Time

Lots of big companies hold **annual** outings for their employees. It's a great way to get out of the office for a while and build a company through team-building or friendly competitions. That's how the Scott Trials originally began. Alfred Angus Scott was a British engineer who designed the Scott motorcycle. His business was called the Scott Engineering Company, and the earliest Scott Trials were part of the company's yearly get-togethers.

Ten-time U.S. Trials champion Geoff Aaron is the first American ever to throw a leg over a trials motorcycle.

Scott used the success of the scramble to help his growing motorcycle company.

Handle With Care

Modern trials competitions remain a popular way of showcasing a rider's skills on a motorcycle. Riders have to complete a course filled with natural obstacles: streams, rock faces, and tricky hills. Observers (sometimes trials are called "observed trials") mark down penalty points to a rider for fouls such as touching the ground with his or her foot, stopping the bike, or failing to complete a section in a specified time. The low score in a trial wins. A modern trials bike is different from a motocross bike because it is lighter and is built with handling as the top priority.

Trials Royalty

Although trials competitions were the forerunners to modern motocross, trials are still popular in Britain. The king of the modern trials riders is England's Dougie Lampkin, who won 12 indoor or outdoor world championships from 1997 to 2003. Lampkin is the son of Martin Lampkin, who was a world champ in 1975. In 2001, Dougie Lampkin was awarded an MBE (Member of the Order of the British Empire) by Queen Elizabeth II.

British Scrambling

The key development in the evolution of motocross came when British riders in the 1920s decided to skip the observation portion of the Trials and focus squarely on completing the course the fastest. The result was the first recognized motocross race, the Southern Scott Scramble, in 1924.

North Against South

The Scott Trial became such a key event in the 1920s that riders in Northern England believed that it proved they were the best around. Naturally, riders in Southern England didn't see it the same way. So one club in the south, the Camberley Club, decided to settle the dispute. It challenged a northern club, the Ilkley Club, to send its riders to the south for a competition. In return, the Camberley Club would send its riders to the Scott Trial. This way, no one from either side could complain that the other simply had a "home-field" advantage.

May the Fastest Bike Win

The Camberley Club originally wanted to call its competition the "Southern Scott Trial." There was just one catch, though. The winner wouldn't be the rider who could complete the course in a certain amount of time with the fewest mistakes. Instead, it would simply be whoever could complete the course the fastest. In that case, then, it wouldn't really be a trial at all. It would be a true race. And if it wasn't a trial, it couldn't be **sanctioned** as one by the national governing body at the time, which was the Auto Cycle Union (ACU). The ACU told the Southern Scott organizers that they had to come up with a new name for their competition. They decided to call it the "Southern Scott Scramble."

Action from the first motocross race in 1924. Riders had to go over or through whatever they encountered...even water!

What's In a Name?

"Scramble," or "scrambling," was the original name for motocross. It came from an off-the-cuff remark that was made when the "Southern Scott" organizers were trying to come up with a name to differentiate their event from the Trials. One of the members of the motorcycle club in Camberley exclaimed, "Whatever we call it, it will be a rare old scramble!"

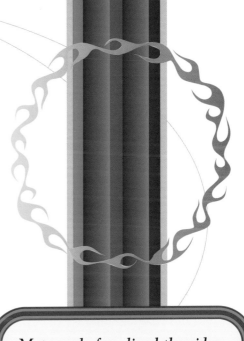

Motorcycle fans lined the sides of hilly English countryside roads to watch the "scramblers" in action.

The Great Race

On Saturday, March 29, 1924, 89 riders and thousands of excited spectators arrived in Camberley for the big race. (Camberley is located about 35 miles (56.33 km) outside of London.) The race would consist of two 25-mile (40.23-km) laps on a course that featured several incredibly steep hills, **bogs**, and other rough areas. Unlike modern motocross, in which everyone starts at the same time, riders started one at a time, one minute apart. The first lap was run in the morning. After everybody had a break for lunch, the second lap was in the afternoon. The rider with the best elapsed time was the winner.

The famous American motorcycle maker Harley-Davidson was part of the early racing scene. U.S. rider F.A. Longman reached 90 mph (144.84 km/h) on this model.

Here to Stay

As it turned out, that winner was a southern rider named Arthur Sparks. The second-place finisher was another southerner, George Dance. The top northerner was Frank Dean, who came in third place. But that didn't solve the argument over who had the best riders, because the 12 northern riders in the race ended up with a better average time. That didn't matter, though. What mattered most was that the competition was a big hit with both riders and fans. At the time of the original Southern Scott Scramble, the idea of a true race instead of a trial was quite a radical departure for the sport of motorcycling. But it quickly caught on. Motocross was born.

Great Britain's riders often sped around flat tracks like this one at Surrey, where F. Dixon models a Harley-Davidson.

Local Knowledge

Arthur Sparks, the winner of the 1924 Southern Scott Scramble, was a local rider from the south. He was a motorcycle mechanic and a member of the Camberley Club. Sparks knew the area and was able to make his way around the 25-mile (40.23-km) course without getting lost. Not everyone did. A sign marking the direction of the course had been accidentally knocked down the day before the race, and many of the riders went off in the wrong direction before getting back on course!

Racing on tracks was a big part of the early motorcycling scene. Riders leaned into turns and had to put down their feet to balance their speeding bikes.

The Sport Evolves

Motocross enjoyed a burst of popularity in Britain in the time period leading up to World War II. Often, tens of thousands of spectators would line the course to watch riders racing on the most popular bikes of the day.

Time to Change

Before motocross could get to that point, however, it needed to make a few adjustments. Remember, the original British scrambling tracks were long courses on which one or two laps made a race. Let's go back to the Southern Scott Scramble in 1924. That was on a track that was 25 miles (40.23 km) long. In addition to the problem the race had with the missing directional sign, fans could only see a small portion of the course. They flocked mostly to one of the famous steep hills and watched riders try to climb the tricky slope.

Wild and Woolly

One of those slopes was nicknamed "Wild and Woolly." It was about 200 yards (182.88m) in length and very, very steep. Most of the riders couldn't make it up the hill without the help of the spectators. Some of the fans would pull the riders up with the help of a rope. Others would push from behind. And yet, some of the riders welcomed the hills on the course because they weren't as tough as the rest of the course. "They weren't nearly as rough or unpredictable as the level stretches through the heath and the harrowing descents that immediately followed the climbs," Bryan Stealey wrote in *Racer X Magazine*.

Not many women raced or rode motorcycles, but those that did often rode together. Here's a fun group: The Motor Maids of America!

A Long Way from Start to Finish

All in all, riders and spectators were thrilled at the new spectacle at the Southern Scott Scramble. But if the sport was to gain popularity, it had to be more spectator-friendly. It had to be more rider-friendly, too, because that first race was a war of **attrition**. That is, it was hard to finish! Of the 89 riders who were entered in the Southern Scott Scramble (80 of them actually started), only 40 of them made it to the finish line of the grueling course.

Smaller is Bigger

Before motocross got bigger, it had to get smaller—smaller courses, that is. The French are credited with changing motocross's format to shorter courses and more laps. Most likely, it was out of necessity. Twenty-five-mile (40.23-km) closed courses weren't easy to find!

(above) Early motorcycle riders depended on leather jackets and helmets for protection on the dirt tracks of England.

(left) A couple of winners from 1935: Freddie Frith (42) and R. Harris (14) after racing at the Junior Manx Grand Prix.

The Chicken or the Egg?

You know the old question, "Which came first, the chicken or the egg?" Well, in motocross, manufacturers began modifying their bikes specifically for the sport in this time period. The bike evolved into a better racing machine. And that leads to a chicken-egg question. Did the improvements in bike manufacturing lead to an increase in the popularity of motocross? Or did an increase in the popularity of motocross make manufacturers create better bikes to keep their old customers and gain new customers?

This photo from 1939 shows just how hard some of the early outdoor courses could be. This rider needed help getting up a steep, muddy hill.

Factory Teams

Bike manufacturers also knew that the best way to attract new customers would be to have spectators see the best riders riding their bikes. So manufacturers, such as the popular BSA or Rudge, began to form "factory teams." Certain riders would only ride certain bikes. The company would pay them to enter races. In return, the company got their bikes advertised on the courses.

Everybody's Happy

This was a good deal for the manufacturers, and it worked out really well for the riders, too. They couldn't make enough money just by racing—the prize money was small, or not at all. Sometimes the winner got a trophy. This was a great way for a good rider to make a living doing something that he loved! The business and racing success of these motorcycle pioneers is still paying off today. Top riders still represent motorcycle brands on the track and in promoting the products—a winning combination for all sides.

By the 1970s, outdoor motorcycle racing had come to America. Here, Rex Staten (top) is shown racing at Daytona International Speedway.

FIM

As motocross spread beyond Great Britain and became a **profession** for motorcycle riders, it was time for a worldwide governing body to oversee the sport. The Fédération Internationale de Motocyclisme (translated from the French, that means the "International Motorcycle Federation") was the international governing body of motorcycle racing. It already included trials and track-racing competitions. Now the Fédération, or FIM for short, officially included motocross among its racing categories, too. FIM was started in Paris in the early 1900s. Britain's Auto Cycle Union, the group that insisted that the organizers of the Southern Scott Trials come up with a new name, was one of the founding members of FIM.

Post-War Boom

The popularity of motocross spread throughout Europe in the post-World War II era. Nations such as Belgium and Sweden became national powers in the sport. In 1947, the first Motocross des Nations was held to crown a world champion.

No Time for Fun

World War II, which was from 1939 to 1945 (and which the United States officially entered in 1941), affected just about everything, including sports. In America, National Football League teams suspended operations, or in cases such as the Philadelphia Eagles and Pittsburgh Steelers, combined operations—they were unofficially called the "Steagles." Major League Baseball teams relied on young players not yet called to fight or on older veterans who were beyond fighting age. Wartime restrictions made travel difficult, and men were needed elsewhere. If they weren't fighting, they were expected to contribute to the war effort in other ways, such as manufacturing. This was especially true in Europe, where the war primarily was waged. England battled to survive an intense bombing campaign from the Germans. There was little time for fun and games, motocross included.

Bikes in Demand

Once the Allies (primarily the United States, Great Britain, and Russia) beat the Axis Powers (primarily Germany, Italy, and Japan), motocross returned in full force in Europe. Even though motorcycles did not play a role in the Second World War like they did in the First World War (see page 7), they were still a popular way to get around—and there were lots of men home from the war who wanted to ride them.

At a 1976 race in Belgium, hometown hero Gaston Rahier leads American Marty Smith around a turn.

World Championship

In 1947, two years after the end of World War II, the national motorcycle federation of the Netherlands hosted the first major international team event. Only three national teams entered the competition: Great Britain, Belgium, and the Netherlands. Predictably, the Great Britain team won, although the Belgians weren't too far behind. Despite the small gathering of teams, the competition soon grew into the most important international motocross event in the world: the Motocross des Nations. Sometimes called the "Olympics of Motocross," it is still held each year.

Flying for the future: Already a world legend in the sport, here's Roger DeCoster (left) zooming through the air along with Vic Allen at a 1974 race in Ohio.

Roger DeCoster

While Great Britain was the dominant country in international competition immediately following World War II, countries such as Belgium and France developed outstanding riders, too. In fact, Belgium's Roger DeCoster was perhaps the greatest motocross rider of the sport's first half-century. He won 36 Motocross Grand Prix titles, was a five-time world champion, and raced for six Belgian teams that won the Motocross des Nations. DeCoster is a member of the Motorcycle Hall of Fame.

Edison Dye Popularizes Motocross in America

Some form of motocross existed in the United States long before Edison Dye came on the scene in the mid-1960s. In fact, "Tourist Trophy" competitions, which were similar to British scrambling, were held as far back as the late 1920s. But Dye popularized the sport by bringing European-style motocross to America.

Ford Tough

What was going on in the United States while motocross was enjoying great popularity in Great Britain and other parts of Europe? Well, during the Great Depression of the 1930s, the motorcycle business almost disappeared—and motocross with it. The Great Depression was a time of financial **hardship** for many Americans. The stock market crashed, and unemployment reached record levels. People still had to get around, but the Ford automobile, which was still fairly new, provided transportation at a price many people could still afford. Motorcycles, which were not as popular as they were in Europe, were considered a luxury, or an entertainment expense.

DeCosters was the first real global superstar of the sport. He won five World Championships and four Trans-AMA titles.

Time of Prosperity

As the memories of World War II gave way to the 1950s, men and women in the United States had more extra income to spend than ever before. Sports, in particular, benefited from the boom, as television brought them into everybody's living room. Sports became more a part of everyday life. Motocross lagged behind television-friendly games such as football, though, which exploded in popularity in the late 1950s and early 1960s. By the mid-1960s, motocross was still a fringe sport, with only pockets of popularity in places such as the Northeast and southern California.

Business Plan

In 1966, though, Edison Dye began taking motocross to a wider audience. Dye was a businessman who had seen the lighter, sleek Husqvarna ("Husky") bikes in motocross action in Europe. He figured he could sell lots of the bikes to Americans, so he worked out a deal with the company to become a distributor in the United States. To promote his product, he paid European Grand Prix champion Torsten Hallman to perform exhibitions on the West Coast. American spectators were amazed at the way Hallman handled a bike. A new era in motocross had begun.

Strong, fast, and creative, Torsten Hallman's many skills revolutionized motocross, especially in the United States. His 1966 tour opened many fans' eyes to what great riders could do.

The "Flying Circus"

Torsten Hallman was such a hit with American motocross fans in 1966 that Edison Dye went back to Europe in 1967. He recruited more riders, even from rival manufacturers, to come to the United States after the European Grand Prix season ended. The resulting American tour was called the "Inter-Am." Unofficially, it was the "Flying Circus." Dye had embarked on a new career as a race promoter.

The AMA

The AMA is the American Motorcyclist Association.
It is the governing body for motocross in America.
The AMA was founded in 1924—coincidentally, the
same year as the first motocross race in Britain.

Winners All Around

Edison Dye's Inter-Am circuit was a big hit.
The European riders liked it because they
supplemented their Grand Prix income—they
were guaranteed a certain amount of money per
race, no matter where they finished in the race.
And they got to see many parts of the United
States, too. Motocross fans liked it because they
got to witness a level of racing never before seen
in America. Edison Dye liked it because he made

a lot of money promoting his tour! Dye was also
trying to sell motorcycles, of course, so the more
people that came, the more bikes he might sell.
But his biggest achievement was getting great
motocross action to a lot of fans.

*By the 1990s, great amateur events were
being run, but they couldn't have made
it without older trailblazers.*

National News

The Inter-Am was not truly a national tour, however. It did not travel to all parts of the country, and it wasn't on TV. Plus, it wasn't exactly a level playing field for Americans riders, either. Though talented, they were awestruck at taking the same track as some of Europe's best riders. Europeans such as Torsten Hallman, Roger DeCoster, Dave Bickers, and Jöel Robert dominated the competition. The experience of the Inter-Am showed the sport's leaders that the United States needed to start its own professional tour. The American Motorcyclist Association (AMA) stepped in to fill that void. The AMA had sanctioned motocross racing since the late 1950s, and began holding amateur and Pro-Am races in the 1960s. But it didn't really show a lot of interest in motocross racing until beginning the Trans-AMA tour in 1970. That tour conflicted with Dye's Inter-Am, and the two clashed. Eventually, though, the Inter-Am folded, and Dye began promoting Trans-AMA races. With the beginning of this important series, the United States finally had its first formal professional championship motocross series.

Pro and Am

Along with the Fédération Internationale de Motocyclisme (FIM) Grand Prix in Europe, the AMA Motocross Championship is one of the top-two series competitions in the world. The AMA also sanctions the most important amateur competition in the United States, the AMA Amateur Motocross Championship.

A champion in Europe in the FIM events, Joël Robert of Belgium also was very successful in American racing competitions.

23

Catching Up to the Europeans

Most people thought that Americans would always lag behind the Europeans in motocross. And despite a couple of second-place finishes in the world competition in the 1970s, that wisdom generally held true. It all changed, though, beginning in 1981.

A Little Help

Credit an assist to Edison Dye for the United States' first major international victory in motocross. Remember Roger DeCoster? He was one of the European stars that Dye brought to the United States as part of his "Flying Circus" in 1967. DeCoster continued to come back to America after the European Grand Prix season when the Trans-AMA series started. DeCoster won several Trans-AMA season championships, and then stayed in the United States to work for the manufacturer Honda. In 1981, he agreed to coach a team of young American riders who would race in Belgium in back-to-back weeks in the Trophée des Nations and the Motocross des Nations (Trophée des Nations is for less powerful bikes).

Sweden's Hakan Carlqvist had great success in the 1980s, but stars of that era were facing a new challenge from the U.S.

Plan B

The American team of Donnie Hansen, Danny LaPorte, Johnny O'Mara, and Chuck Sun essentially was a backup team after the original racers were pulled from the competition by their bike manufacturers. The squad was given little chance of posting a decent showing, let alone winning. The Americans not only won, but they routed the field in a stunning victory. The next week, the four riders proved it was no fluke by edging Great Britain in the Motocross des Nations.

Passing Lane

The United States had arrived on the world motocross stage. But it was more than an indicator that the United States had caught up to the Europeans in motocross—the Americans had flat out blown past them! That's because the 1981 competition marked the first of 13 consecutive Motocross des Nations championships for the United States. The streak didn't end until Great Britain won in 1994. The Americans have won several times since, too, including their third title in a row in 2007.

Independence Day

As a team, the United States arrived with its victory in 1981. But even before that, Gary Bailey served notice of the Americans' coming strength with a victory at Saddleback Park in Orange County, California, in 1969. Fittingly, it came on the Fourth of July! Bailey was racing against several notable Europeans, including world champion Arne Kring of Sweden, in Edison Dye's Inter-Am series. No American had ever won a race against the Europeans before. But with the crowd chanting "Bay-Lee! Bay-Lee!" Bailey won the second moto (motocross races include two runs called motos) and took the overall victory.

The Peter Chamberlain Trophy is one of the most important prizes in motocross.

Made in America: Supercross

The popularity of motocross has given rise to a uniquely American version of the sport: supercross. Supercross is what its organizers got when they scaled down the natural terrain of a motocross course into a man-made course that could fit the dimensions of an NFL-style stadium.

The Short Version

Contrary to popular belief, supercross was not invented in America. Indeed, stadium-style motocross was tried in Paris, France, way back in the late 1940s. But it wasn't until the early 1970s in Los Angeles, California, that supercross found its own identity. Organizer Mike Goodwin believed he could bring motocross to a whole new audience by holding an event in the comfort of a large stadium and promoting it with the **zeal** of a rock concert promoter. He called it the "Super Bowl of Motocross," which was a mouthful! Advertisers and journalists quickly shortened it to "Supercross." On July 8, 1972, more than 28,000 fans watched the first supercross event at the Los Angeles Memorial Coliseum.

Normally the home of NASCAR racing, Daytona is also the site of an annual motocross event. Here's Australian Michael Byrne at the 2007 Daytona SX.

Not Just a Fad

The next year, more than 38,000 fans were on hand in the Coliseum for the second "Super Bowl of Motocross." Since then, this form of motocross has soared like Ricky Carmichael off the whoops at the supercross track at Angel Stadium in Anaheim, California! The AMA sanctions an entire supercross schedule, with annual stops at other notable indoor and outdoor stadiums such as AT&T Park in San Francisco, Qualcomm Field in San Diego, Reliant Stadium in Houston, the Georgia Dome in Atlanta, the Metrodome in Minneapolis, and more football and baseball stadiums all over the country. **Arenacross** is an even further downsized version of supercross and is raced in indoor basketball and hockey arenas.

Scoring Decision

One key difference between motocross and supercross is in the scoring. The winner of a motocross event has the best **aggregate** score of two runs (motos). But the winner of a supercross event is whoever crosses the finish line first in the "Main Event," which is the final race. Riders make it to the Main Event through a series of qualifying races leading up to the finals.

Daytona!

The **precursor** to the supercross event in Los Angeles in 1972 was a motocross race at the famous Daytona International Speedway—stock-car racing's most famous site—in 1971. Organizers there built a motocross course on the infield of the famous superspeedway. Spectators watched from ground level. It was such a hit that the course was moved in front of the grandstand the following year to accommodate more fans. Supercross has been run annually at Daytona ever since on a track that was designed by former motocross star Gary Bailey.

Fans are getting an up-close look at the start of this supercross race. The white gates in front of the riders will drop at the same time, and the race will begin.

The American Stars

Forty or so years ago, the superstars of motocross were all from Europe: Sweden's Torsten Hallman, Belgium's Roger DeCoster, and more. But the spectacular growth of motocross in the 1980s and 1990s has led to the evolution of America's own superstars in the sport.

Jeremy McGrath

If you like to play motocross or supercross video games, you probably know all about Jeremy McGrath. He was certainly the most recognizable American motorcycle star of the 1990s—and maybe ever. McGrath was not only a great champion, but he was a great showman, too. He brought a style and flair to the sport never before seen from an American rider. McGrath won an AMA-record 72 supercross titles and seven season championships. He was great outside the stadiums, too, where he posted 17 AMA motocross victories. McGrath retired in 2003 and was only 31 years old when he was inducted into the Motorcycle Hall of Fame that year.

Ricky Carmichael (top) and Jeremy McGrath (No. 2) are America's greatest motocrossers.

Ricky Carmichael

They called Ricky Carmichael the "G.O.A.T." That wasn't a bad nickname. It was an **acronym** that stood for "Greatest of All Time." Jeremy McGrath fans might think their guy deserves that title, but there is hardly any major championship that Carmichael failed to win before retiring at just 27 years old in 2007. Carmichael's 150 career victories are more than any other rider in motocross history. In seven seasons from 2000 to 2006, he won all seven AMA motocross and five AMA supercross series championships. Don't be surprised if one day you find Ricky's name among the top NASCAR drivers. Since his retirement from motocross, he has gone into stock-car racing.

James Stewart Jr.

James Stewart Jr. is better known to his fans as "Bubba." Before his career is over, they may be calling him the best American rider ever. He began riding at a very young age, inspired by his father, a motorcycle fan. By the time he was a teenager, he was one of the top amateur riders in the nation, regularly taking high places at AMA events. In fact, before turning pro at age 16 in 2002, Bubba surpassed Ricky Carmichael as the top AMA amateur rider ever. Since then, Bubba has continued his winning ways, taking several regional and class supercross titles. After battling illness and injury in 2006, he broke through to the top in 2007, winning 13 events and his first AMA Supercross national championship, before winning the 2007 FIM WSXGP Supercross championship. Stewart was also the first African American rider to accomplish that feat.

AMA Champions (since 2000)

Supercross

Year	Rider	Hometown	Bike
2007	James Stewart Jr.	Haines City, FL	Kawasaki
2006	Ricky Carmichael	Havana, FL	Suzuki
2005	Ricky Carmichael	Havana, FL	Suzuki
2004	Chad Reed	Dade City, FL	Yamaha
2003	Ricky Carmichael	Havana, FL	Honda
2002	Ricky Carmichael	Havana, FL	Honda
2001	Ricky Carmichael	Havana, FL	Kawasaki
2000	Jeremy McGrath	Menifee, CA	Yamaha

Motocross

Year	Rider	Hometown	Bike
2007	Grant Langston	Clermont, FL	Yamaha
2006	Ricky Carmichael	Havana, FL	Suzuki
2005	Ricky Carmichael	Havana, FL	Suzuki
2004	Ricky Carmichael	Havana, FL	Honda
2003	Ricky Carmichael	Havana, FL	Honda
2002	Ricky Carmichael	Havana, FL	Honda
2001	Ricky Carmichael	Havana, FL	Kawasaki
2000	Ricky Carmichael	Havana, FL	Kawasaki

A Sport for the 2000s

As motocross' popularity continues to grow, a whole new generation has been introduced to the sport through the X Games. Motocross has been part of the Summer X Games since 1999 and has given rise to stars such as Travis Pastrana, Tommy Clowers, and Kenny Bartram.

Star Power

It's X Games 12 at the Staples Center in Los Angeles, and more than 13,000 spectators are on their feet. Those fans include the likes of actress Sandra Bullock and her husband, *Monster Garage* TV host Jesse James. They've already seen some incredible tricks like a "Nac-Nac backflip" from Mat Rebaud. But now they are cheering loudly as Travis Pastrana, the best motocross rider in X Games history, has signaled his intention to make X Games history. He's going to try a double backflip. Pastrana takes off down the ramp and flies through the air. It's an almost impossible trick, but he does it! He sticks the landing, with both tires on his motorcycle touching down at once and bringing him solidly back to the ground. The crowd goes crazy!

A New Kind of Motocross

That's the kind of wild action you see in motocross competitions at the X Games. It's an altogether different kind of motocross competition in which riders compete in events such as freestyle, **step up**, and best trick. In 2006, Pastrana won three gold medals at the X Games.

Freestyle tricks have all sorts of cool names. Here's FX ace Ronnie Faisst doing a gravity-defying "Indian Air."

Time to Step Up

Motocross at the X Games is mostly associated with the freestyle and best-trick events. Those are the real crowd pleasers, and the ones in which riders can exhibit their own personalities and styles. But one of the most challenging events is called step up. In step up, riders have to clear a horizontal bar that is raised higher and higher each round. Once a rider fails to completely clear a bar, he is out of the competition. The bar is raised six inches each round until one rider remains: the champion.

The X Games features a supermoto event that combines street and dirt racing. Jeff Ward (1), a racing legend, shows his stuff at the X Games.

Moto X is the latest addition to the list of freestyle events at the X Games. Here's Travis Pastrana flying high on his Suzuki.

Glossary

acronym A word that is made up from the first letters of a group of words

aggregate The sum, or total

amateur Someone who does a job or plays a sport just for fun, not for money

annual Happening each year

attrition A reduction in size

berm The slanted bank of dirt that gathers in the turns of MX tracks

bogs Wet, spongy stretches of ground

distinct Different in nature

exported Sent to other countries

hairpin turn A very tight, almost 180-degree, turn

hardship Difficulty

precursor Something that comes before something else

profession A way to make a living

sanctioned Given permission for

sophisticated Complex, or advanced

zeal Enthusiasm

Index

32

Printed in the U.S.A.